Why the F**k Didn't I Learn This in School?
How to Build and Fix Credit

Antoine Rucker

© Copyright 2020

All rights reserved.

The contents of this book may not be reproduced, duplicated, or transmitted without direct written permission from the author. Under no circumstances will any legal responsibility or blame be held against the publisher for any reparation, damages, or monetary loss due to the information herein, either directly or indirectly.

Legal Notice:

This book is copyright protected. This is only for personal use. You cannot amend, distribute, sell, use, quote or paraphrase any part of the content within this book without the consent of the author.

Contents

INTRODUCTION 1

CHAPTER 1 3

UNDERSTANDING CREDIT REPAIR 3

CREDIT REPAIR AT WORK 4
CREDIT REPAIR OFFERINGS 5
THE REALITIES 6

CHAPTER 2 11

CREDIT SCORE 11

THE IMPORTANCE OF CREDIT SCORE 12
HOW CREDIT SCORE WORK 13
CALCULATING YOUR CREDIT SCORE 14
GOOD CREDIT SCORE 16

CHAPTER 3 17

WHAT DETERMINES YOUR CREDIT SCORE 17

FACTORS AFFECTING CREDIT SCORE 17

CHAPTER 4 21

UNDERSTANDING CREDIT UTILIZATION 21

WHAT IS CREDIT UTILIZATION? 21
HOW CREDIT UTILIZATION AFFECTS YOUR CREDIT SCORE 22
MANAGING YOUR CREDIT UTILIZATION 22

CHAPTER 5 26

CREDIT REPORT 26

HOW CREDIT REPORT WORK 26
CREDIT HISTORY 28
HOW TO GET CREDIT REPORTS 30
READING A CREDIT REPORT RIGHTLY 31
IMPORTANCE OF CREDIT REPORTS 33

CHAPTER 6 — 35

REPAIRING YOUR CREDIT — 35

The Steps To Repair Your Credit — 36
Using Goodwill Letter — 42
When you need a Goodwill Letter — 43
Writing your Goodwill Letter — 45
Sample Goodwill letter — 47

CHAPTER 7 — 49

MANAGING YOUR CREDIT CARD — 49

Secured Credit Card — 49
How Secured Credit Cards Work — 50
Unsecured Credit Card — 50
How Unsecured Credit Cards Work — 51
Choosing the Right Credit Card — 51
Using Your Credit Card Rightly — 54

CHAPTER 8 — 59

IDENTITY THEFT 59

Preventing Identity Theft 60
Dealing with Identity Theft 61

CHAPTER 9 64

DISPUTING INADEQUACIES IN YOUR REPORT 64

How Do You Order for a Free Credit report? 65
Correct Inadequacies in Credit Report 68

Conclusion 74

INTRODUCTION

The American population is growing daily, with an increase in household debt. More people are falling into the pit of debt, and they seek means of relieving themselves of the challenges of credit they are in. Bad debt has its toil on every individual. It takes away the opportunity of being granted loans or insurance at the best rate.

The issues of life are enough to make one consider life as being extremely stressful. But when bad credit joins this reality, one will likely think that the world is not a place for him or her. More people have fallen victim to the several purported credit repair companies who make promises they can never keep.

The truth is that you don't need the help of a "professional" to repair your credit. All you've got to do is take up the mantle on yourself and bear the responsibility. With the right information at your fingertips, you will deal with your credit faster and easier than you may think.

In this guide, you will learn about the intricacies of how to manage your credit and build your score. I have compiled information that will help you prevent identity theft, which may hamper your credit report. And there are sample letters of goodwill and dispute letter for you to handle your credit report and make it have a positive effect on your credit score.

CHAPTER 1
UNDERSTANDING CREDIT REPAIR

Credit repair has to do with the process of you working on your poor credit stance. Usually, people suffer from bad debt, which comes as a result of several reasons. Credit repair doesn't have to be a complex adventure. It may be as simple as you disputing wrong information with credit agencies or you identifying instances of identity theft to prevent or forestall any possible damages that often come with it. Credit repair involves you working on your credit report to make it have a positive effect on your credit score. And it is also possible for you to handle your credit repair from the angle of setting the right budgeting to resolve certain financial issues.

Since credit repair is an act of correction, it, therefore, means that something is wrong. You may contact a company to help you contact the credit bureaus and identify the discrepancies in your credit report. The company represents you and demand that every error be adjusted and removed where necessary. But, it is best you do your credit repair yourself. While it may be time-consuming, it is worth the stress.

Credit Repair At Work

It is common to find companies saying they can clean bad credit reports and that they can correct errors in the information that may appear on a credit report. The truth is, all of these steps take time and effort. Note that erroneous information on your credit report cannot be removed by a third party. It has to be done by the credit bureau. You or any company that is acting in your capacity can do is to dispute inaccurate and misrepresented information in your credit report.

As an individual, you are entitled to a free report on your credit once a year from each of the recognized credit reporting agencies. Identifying the areas of your credit report that have inaccurate information is one effective means of repairing your credit. There are other possible means, such as correcting your credit usage and credit activities. These activities include putting your payment history into considerations, as it determines a lot about your creditworthiness. You've got to take decisive steps that will help you improve your payment schedule.

Credit Repair Offerings

Over the years, credit repair has taken a significant aspect of our financial terrain. There are lots of businesses coming up with the claim that they help with credit repair. It is possible to see some of these companies helping consumers with their credit needs, but many of these companies don't give unquestionable results. There are times you've got to bring legal and financial expertise together. The degree of your financial mess determines what you will need to do to get your credit cleaned. While disputing works in some cases, for some, you've got to involve the service of a professional to intervene.

Note that working with a credit repair company comes with its fees, which are often in two forms – the initial setup fee and a monthly service fee. Depending on the company, you may have to pay between $10 and $100 for the initial fee, while the monthly service is from $30 to $100. Paying shouldn't come first, that is, if you are considering working with a company, which is not necessary. You've got to consider what you will get in return for your payment. There is nothing a credit repair company can do for you that you cannot do for yourself. You've only got to create the time and put your all into it.

The Realities

Living with bad credit makes life difficult for anyone. More companies have now made a person's creditworthiness a criterion for deciding whether they can transact with the person or not—the same thing for lenders. No one wants to lend his or her money to someone whose credit score is low. And if there is an offer for you, it will come with exorbitant fees. This explains why consumers are after the repair of their credit. But with this action comes some realities. Let me take you through them.

You can handle your credit repair

Don't be deceived into thinking that credit repair is for some set of professionals only. Credit repair companies may be an option for some people if those people are too busy with their schedule that they don't have the opportunity to spare the required time and effort needed to repair their credit. But note that if it is on the basis of competence, you've got nothing to fear. Credit repair is not something meant for some professionals. With the right information, you can get the repair of your credit done. So, there is no service a credit report company wants to render to you that you cannot do yourself. When you handle your credit repair, you are able to save money for yourself. Also, it gives you access to manage your money and credit history better.

The focus is on your credit report

Many people believe that repairing their credit has to do with them working on their credit score. The truth is, you are more concerned with your credit report. Your credit score is a result of your credit report. So, the trick is for you to handle your report. When your report is void of any inaccuracies, your credit score will be fine.

Handling inaccurate or wrong information is demanding

Note that if your credit repair process has to do with the removal of inaccurate information, then you have got a tough path to tread. Inaccurate information affects the credit score of a person negatively. But the credit reporting agencies can remove it after their thorough investigation into it. Removing inaccurate information comes with strategies that I will share with you later.

Credit Repair Companies Cannot Be Trusted

Don't make the mistake of trusting credit repair companies. It is so easy to find many of these companies giving you lofty promises of what they don't have the capacity to give. They are usually after the fees they charge, and this is why you see them charge upfront fees but fail to deliver. Although federal law prohibits this, many consumers don't know about this. Credit repair companies that are not trustworthy will request you to make an upfront payment, promise you a certain amount of credit score, make a promise to delete information from your credit report, won't tell you about your right to dispute inaccurate information, and they are likely to tell you to waive your rights under the Credit Repair Organizations Act. All of these are pointers that you are in the wrong place.

Credit Repair takes time

Credit repair is not something you do overnight. It takes a whole lot of time to build a crashed credit reputation. It may take you a few months to make the right adjustments. And within these months, you've got to work hard on building your credit by taking the right steps. As you retrace your steps to build your credit report, certainly, you will discover an improvement in your credit.

Your Financial Habits Matter

It is not enough to use the credit repair tactics you learned only. You've got to let go of some bad habits. That you've built your credit report doesn't mean it is not going to crash again if you fail to maintain it. So, to avoid the possibility of you losing all that you have, ensure you keep the right attitude. Maintaining good financial habits will help you work on your credit and maintain it continually. Note that your credit crashed in the first place probably because of your bad financial habits, so when you are able to correct the issues, ensure you don't go back to the same habits.

CHAPTER 2
CREDIT SCORE

A credit score works just like the grading system of students. Just that, in this case, it is a three-digit number. A credit score ranges from 300 to 850, and it is used to show a person's level of credit risk and the likelihood of paying a credit. The higher your credit score, the better you will be perceived by lenders, financial institutions, and other businesses as a borrower. Credit scores are calculated based on the information that is available in a person's credit report. This information includes your payment history, how long your credit history has been existing, the amount you owe, among others. A higher score means you are a responsible borrower that can be trusted with more credit, while a lower score means otherwise.

The most commonly used credit score model was created by the Fair Isaac Corporation (FICO), and this model is used by many financial institutions. There are other available scoring models, and they use some different data to reach their results. Credit score ranges within the following:

Score	Grade
800 - 850	Excellent
740 - 799	Very good
670 - 739	Good
580 - 669	Fair
300 - 579	Poor

The Importance of Credit Score

One of the many questions that should come to mind about a credit score is that, why is it so important? Having a high credit score will give you a favorable stance before lenders as they are ready to offer you favorable terms such as a low-interest rate on loan.

Note that lenders and creditors use different types of credit scores based on their industry. An auto lender may be interested in using a credit score that is more focused on your payment history in order to grant you an auto loan. Also, the scoring model used for your score varies the scores. Also, the credit bureau that furnishes your credit report data may be a cause of differences in your credit score. The reason for this is that all creditors don't give their reports to all the three credit licensed bureaus: Experian, Equifax, and TransUnion.

How Credit Score Work

Your credit score has a tremendous influence on your financial life. In the present time, your credit score is used to determine your creditworthiness by lenders. You may be considered a *subprime borrower* if your credit score is lower than 640. When considered as a *subprime borrower,* lenders tend to charge a higher rate of interest on a *subprime mortgage,* which is usually higher than that of a normal mortgage. The high rate is used as a form of compensation for the risk they are bearing. Also, you are most likely going to have to pay within a short time frame.

However, having a credit score of 700 and above places you ahead of every requirement of any lender. Creditors will be willing to give you credit with a low-interest rate. And if you have got a score that is above

800, every creditor will be after you as an excellent borrower.

Your credit score determines the amount of initial deposit you may be required to make for you to obtain certain items such as a smartphone, pay for rent, and more.

Calculating Your Credit Score

The calculation of your credit score is done by the analysis of the data contained in your credit report. The standard factors considered in calculating your score are five, and they include:

Payment history: The history of how you have paid so far takes 35% of your credit score calculation. It reflects your responsiveness to the payment of your bills. Also, it shows whether you miss your payment at times or not. If all of these are positive, your score will be affected positively.

Your existing credit: the amount you owe on your credit cards makes up 30% of your credit score calculation. This looks at how much you owe entirely. It looks at the types of accounts you have and their numbers. It looks at how much you owe and the amount you have available by comparing them. If you have a high balance and you've used up your credit cards, your credit score will be lowered, but with a small balance on your cards, your score will be raised.

Your credit history length: this takes 15% of your credit score total calculations. People with longer years of credit history with timely payments enjoy a high score. Lack of credit history will affect your credit score.

Your account type: The type of account you open takes up 10% of your credit score calculation. So, if you have many accounts, such as a home loan, retail, and credit card accounts, you will have the chance to increase your credit score.

Your credit activities: Your credit score is calculated by looking at your recent credit activities. Applying to several accounts could mean you have challenges with your finances. And this can lower your credit score. But if you have a loan that has been for a long time and you have always paid at the right time, when you have financial issues, your score will not be affected. It pays to pay your credit early and at the right time.

Good Credit Score

A good credit score is a score you need to enjoy the benefits available in the financial industry. As a consumer, you shouldn't obtain a loan that will take forever to repay. However, if your credit score is bad, you would be forced to pay more in interest than others. With an excellent credit score of 850, your financial goals become easy and possible to achieve more. A good credit score gives you access to the best credit cards, competitive loan rates, and mortgages. All of these will save you cost over a period. When your credit score builds confidence in you in the hearts of lenders, it is a good credit score.

CHAPTER 3
WHAT DETERMINES YOUR CREDIT SCORE

A credit score is a certain number used by money lenders to determine how likely it is for you to pay your debt. Your credit score is totally built on your credit history, which consists of the total number of open accounts, total levels of debt, repayment history, and other factors. Your credit score ranges from 300 to 850. A good credit score is important to a great financial life because it essentially determines how less of a credit risk you are. This is why it is necessary to have a decent credit score to increase your access to financial aid. Your credit score doesn't exist alone. It is a result of some underground activities being played by different factors.

Factors Affecting Credit Score

As your financial life grows, so does your credit score. It is important to know what factors are influencing your credit score to be able to make changes over time. Here are some possible factors that might be influencing your credit score:

Payment History: This is considered the most important aspect of your credit score. It takes only one missed payment to alter your credit score because money lenders want to ascertain that you can pay a debt on time when they want to lend you money. Serious payment history such as bankruptcy, repossessions, tax liens, or foreclosures can greatly affect your credit score and make it really difficult to get financial aid from money lenders. Your payment history takes a sum of 35% of your FICO score, which is the credit score utilized by most lenders. It is, therefore, very important that you maintain a good payment history.

Credit Utilization: A credit utilization ratio is measured by dividing the total current credit by the total number of your current credit limit. It is the percentage of the borrowers' total available credit that is being used. This ratio examines how much of the at hand credit you are using and provides a snap of how trustworthy you are with your non-cash funds. A person's credit utilization ratio goes up and down during payments and purchases. Your credit utilization sums up a total of 30% of your FICO Score. It is important to be attentive to your credit utilization ratio and ensure it is low, as a high ratio can influence your credit score negatively.

Credit history length: Your credit history length takes 15% of your FICO score. Your credit history length is the duration of the period your account has been open for. The longer your account has been opened, the better for you, especially if you have a good payment history. The 15% of your FICO score include your oldest credit account, the age of your newest credit card, and the average of all your credit cards. The credit scoring algorithm measures the average of how long all your accounts have been opened. The average age of all your accounts is known as 'credit age.'

Credit Mix: The credit mix takes 10% of your FICO score. People with high credit scores tend to have multiple portfolios of credit accounts, which range from a student loan, credit card, car loan, and others. A credit score takes into consideration credit mixes in order to have a detailed profile of a person's payment history, reliance, and the tendency to effectively manage various credit types. Although having a mix of different accounts can influence your credit score positively, it is advisable for you to not opt to create accounts you do not need because opening new accounts can also affect the length of your consumer credit history and money owed.

New Credit: This consists of the accounts you have just opened, and the numbers of hard inquiries money lenders make when you apply for credit. It takes up 10% of your FICO score. However, it is important to note that the presence of too many accounts or inquiries can connote risk and influence your credit score negatively.

These aforementioned factors are the five major items that can influence your credit score. Taking into consideration these factors would help you track and monitor your financial habits that relate to your credit score. When all these factors are considered, you will be able to improve your credit score so it can work to your advantage.

CHAPTER 4
UNDERSTANDING CREDIT UTILIZATION

A credit card gives you the opportunity to establish a credit record and a credit score. However, having a good credit score is highly dependent on your credit utilization ratio, so it is important for you to have a clear understanding of what it is and how you can manage it effectively for it to work well for you.

What is Credit Utilization?

A credit utilization ratio is the outstanding credit balance on your credit card. Your credit utilization ratio calculates the amount of available credit you are making use of.

How Credit Utilization Affects Your Credit Score

The FICO scoring model examines your credit utilization in two different parts. It measures your credit utilization for all your credit cards separately and calculates your total credit utilization. High credit utilization has the tendency to affect your credit score. For instance: if you have a $400 balance when you have a credit limit of $1000, your credit utilization for that particular credit card is 40%. Your credit utilization ratio is calculated by dividing your credit card balance by your credit limit, then multiply by 100. When your credit utilization percentage is low, it influences your credit score positively because it depicts that you have the ability to manage your money effectively by spending lesser than your credit limit.

Managing Your Credit Utilization

Now that the importance of credit Utilization has been established, let's take a look at how you can manage your credit score to achieve good results.

Spread out Your Charges Over Different Cards

Spreading out your balances over different cards instead of a balance that utilizes more than 30% of your limit on one card; however, this might not always be effective as some models examine your total usage on several cards to calculate your credit utilization rate.

Make Timely Payments

Observe the Date you make your card payment every month and figure out when your card issuer reports information to credit bureaus. If your balance is high at this period (which usually occurs a few days to the billing cycle), it is very likely that your credit utilization will be high as well. The solution to this is to ensure that your balance is low on the day the billing cycle ends.

Request an Increase in Card Limit from your Card Issuer

If you have a card limit with $10000 limits and you spend $5000 out of it, your utilization rate would be 50%. If you ask your creditor to increase your card limit to about $20000 when you have an increase in income, this would automatically reduce your card utilization, which would greatly improve your credit score. The downside of this, however, is the fact that credit bureaus can make an investigation and realize you have requested additional credit, which can lead to a hard inquiry on your credit report. Note that if you change a job that does not pay as much as the previous job, your card issuer can make a reduction in your card limit; therefore, before you ask for an increase in credit limit from your card issuer, ensure you consider your present circumstances and see if you would make a good case.

Pay Your Credit Cards Twice Each Month

This is most likely the cheapest way to ensure your credit utilization is low; when you make a mid-month payment, this will pay the card back to a level that occurs below 30%.

The aforementioned are some ways you can manage your credit utilization in a way that your credit utilization ratio reduces and upgrades your credit score. The highlight, however, is the fact that high credit utilization will not impact your credit score negatively forever. The moment your credit card balance reduces, or there is an increase in your credit limit, your credit utilization will reduce, and your credit score will increase.

CHAPTER 5
CREDIT REPORT

A credit report is a comprehensive analysis containing the main points about how an individual has managed his credit accounts. It shows all kinds of accounts operated and how the payment has been carried out. It also contains other information that was reported to credit bureaus by the money lenders and by entities that rendered services to the individual. The credit report holds all essential financial information pertaining to an individual.

How Credit Report Works

A credit report is the full explanation of individual credit history, which is made ready by a credit bureau. This detailed information, which determines how an individual is viewed by financial institutions, is provided in the credit report. Every credit report has four essential parts, which are:

First Part

It contains the summary of an individual's personal facts, which includes social security number, past and present addresses, and job history. The information provided in this part can differ on the customer's name and social security number if it is deliberately reported wrong by the consumer, or it was erroneously reported by the lender.

Second part

This contains the majority of the reports, and it contains a full explanation about the tradelines, lines of credit that recognizes when an individual is accepted for credit. It stores all activity in an account as well as reporting to a credit reporting agency.

Third part

This part contains all public records ascribed to matters of the law. It reports on all pending legal actions of an individual without mentioning or highlighting previous charges.

Fourth part

This shows the breakdown of all the entities that have requested to see the individual's credit report because of an event such as an application for credit, personal loans, insurance policy, etc. The credit bureaus are paid for such reports, which explain the revenue generated by the bureau.

Credit History

This is the record or account of an individual's ability to pay back debts. It reflects the prior activities in regards to taking up the responsibility of debt payment. The information present in an individual's credit history determines whether or not the individual has credit extended to the individual by mortgage lenders and credit card companies. Individual credit history is utilized to determine the FICO score, which is the standard measurement used to determine a person's credit score.

Creditors and money lenders review an applicant's history by checking several factors, including: recent actions on how long the credit has been opened and in use. They also examine and study the style and frequency of paying back debts over a long period.

A good credit history yields many financial benefits. For example, the interest rate is significantly lower in purchasing commodities; lower rates are paid on loans, insurance, etc.

Negative credit history can still be improved to become positive over time; according to experts, it is advisable to pay back debts in series instead of at once. This act shows responsibility and dependable character. You can do this to pay off both loans and the minimum amount in installment to reduce debt with time.

Possible but not actual borrowers with no credit history, e.g., young adults that are college-bound, may encounter objections in securing approval for considerable leases or finances due to uncertainties about their abilities to make payments when it is due. Their credit histories can be built by applying for a credit card or by obtaining a personal loan with little available balance to show how well they can manage little debts before taking on huge debts.

How To Get Credit Reports

In the United States, there are three major credit reporting bureaus that are responsible for collating and organizing individuals' credit information and making it available to creditors, lenders, and other organizations that may request it in order to enable them to make decisions on granting loans. These bureaus are:

1) Equifax

2) Experian

3) TransUnion

The bureaus collate data concerning every individual's financial information and their bill-paying pattern to formulate a unique credit report for each individual. Despite receiving similar information, they still produce reports with little difference.

An amendment to the Federal Fair Care Reporting Act (FCRA) allows all citizens to get a credit report from the three credit bureaus without charge. To monitor against errors in your credit reports, you've got the right to order a report from each of the three bureaus once a year. However, to make it work well for you, you can just request a report from each of the bureaus every four months. It will help you monitor your credit report and identify any discrepancy in it before it is too late. If you have been a victim of identity theft, you should order your reports frequently. Federal laws also permit individuals who face legal action by the companies to receive a free credit report.

Reading A Credit Report Rightly

There are common errors that can be found on the credit reports. To avoid legal actions, disputes, loss of opportunity due to errors on your credit reports, pay attention to the following points as you read your credit report.

1) ***Identity error:*** Names may be misspelled wrongly. It is also possible for the bureaus to mix up your account with another's identity who answers a similar name as you. Check out for wrong contact addresses, wrong phone numbers, and wrong social security number or if you have been a victim of identity theft where unauthorized transactions have been carried out using your personal details.
2) ***Repetition errors:*** When a creditor changes his/her name, the same debt could be written multiple times under different names, so make sure you check and confirm the numbers.
3) ***Accounting errors:*** Calculation of your balance may be wrong, or you may have a wrong credit limit, which could hurt your credit score or lead to the payment of over-limit fees
4) ***Financial arrangement error:*** Wrong dates which make on-time payments appear as default payment, wrong information on whether an account is open or closed.

All of these are possible errors that may appear on your credit report. If any of them show up, your score will be affected negatively. However, it is possible to correct these errors, and once they are rectified, your score will return to its normal status.

Importance Of Credit Reports

Credit reports are the sole determinant of the financial reliability of every individual. It's the only way to

Identify individuals with good financial responsibility skills. A credit score is the numerical representation of the financial responsibilities of individuals according to the credit reports and other sources of information that can predict future delinquencies

The report determines the FICO score, which selectively allows individuals with a good credit report to represents a lower risk to money lenders. A good FICO score is a major prerequisite to get quicker loans, better interest rates on loans, among others.

A Poor negative report, however, affects your credit score, your chances of getting good mortgage rates, affects job applications, the chances of getting good accommodation, credit card approval, insurance policies, T.V., internet, and phone services. Since credit scores are the major determinant of the services received, the higher the credit scores, the better the services you will receive.

By improving your credit report, you will definitely change your credit score. And to do all of these, you've got to keep paying your bills on time, use your credit cards responsibly, and reduce your debt. Being credit worth is a function of having a positive credit report.

CHAPTER 6
REPAIRING YOUR CREDIT

Repairing your credit has to do with two possibilities – making corrections to improve your credit report or taking up a new financial lifestyle that will affect your credit report and influence your credit score. When your credit score is repaired, you will experience an improved credit score, which will qualify you for lower interest rates on loans, and you will get access to better loan terms. Repairing your credit is not impossible. It only requires a considerable amount of work from you. You don't have to follow the advertisement you've seen on how to repair your credit card. No one is a professional at repairing your credit. No one can improve your credit score. You can only take steps to correct every error that may have impacted your credit score wrongly. And for this, you don't need anybody's help. Below are the steps you need to take to repair your credit.

The Steps To Repair Your Credit

Always evaluate your credit report

The basic foundation of your credit score is your credit report. If your report is faulty, then your score is faulty. You've got to ensure that your credit report carries the right information about your credit history. And to do this, review your report. You have access to your credit report from the three credit bureaus – Equifax, TransUnion, and Experian. These agencies are required by the law to give you a copy of your credit report once a year. So, you can get your report from these bureaus. Ensure you go through your report at least three times annually. The trick is for you to request your report every four months from each of the credit bureaus.

Identify and Dispute Negative Entries

Repairing your credit score has to do with you disputing the negative piece of information contained in your credit report. This could be done by submitting a dispute letter to the credit bureaus. The reason you have to analyze your credit report is so that you can pinpoint the issues that are available in your credit report. In your credit report, look out for derogatory marks such as judgments and collection accounts. You will most likely see at least one collection account on your report. It may be from your health care providers. Errors in your report may come from any of the three credit bureaus. Disputing any error will boost your profile. Initiating a dispute means you want the credit bureaus to investigate the discrepancies in your report and find a solution.

Correct Late Payment

Late-payment entries in your credit report will place you in a bad position. It is possible for your mortgage lender to report a late payment by mistake. It is even possible for a credit card provider to make such a grave mistake. When such happens, you have the right to dispute the entry and ask for a correction to be made.

Build up your credit Limits

In a previous chapter, I showed you how credit utilization impacts your credit score. You've got to consider the ratio of available credit to the credit you used. This ratio always makes a big difference. If you are carrying a balance of over 50% of your credit that is available will affect your credit score negatively. At the same time, if you use up your cards, your score will go down the drain. So, it is advised that you pay down your balances or you increase the limit of your credit. For example, if you owe $5000 on a card that has a limit of $10,000, if you get the limit increased to $12,500, you will experience an improvement in your ratio.

You don't have to pull any special stunts to get this done. All you need is to call and make your request nicely. If your payment history is fine and not filled with defaults, many credit card companies will be glad to increase your card limit. Having a higher balance also benefit them. However, ensure you don't make use of the additional credit. Using it will take you back to the initial position.

Set up a new Credit card Account

When you open a new account, your credit utilization ratio will increase. Just make sure you don't have any balance on the new card. When you open a new account, it is essential that you go for a card that doesn't attract an annual fee. When you are getting a new credit card, ensure you are smart. You are not trying to get more cash. You only need to improve your credit score. So, if you know that you will want to use up a balance on your new account, don't bother to open a new one,

Settle you outstanding balances ahead

While this may sound funny, since the reason you are repairing your credit is to have access to borrow more money among others, and if you've enough to pay your balance ahead, you don't have to borrow, yet. It is a good move to pay off your outstanding balances. When you decrease the percentage of your available credit used, your credit score will be positively impacted. So, you may just look for a new workable budget plan that will allow you to pay off your balances. This strategy may be tough for you as a short-term method, but if you are considering a long-term move to improve your credit score, it is an awesome step for you to take. Using this strategy will help to increase your credit score and as well as reduce your interest.

Deal with new credit accounts with high-interest

One of the central factors that affect your credit report is the age of your credit. Ensure you are paying off accounts with a high-interest rate. Go for the latest accounts and follow by the age of the accounts. When you pay off the newest accounts, you are increasing the average length of credit, and it will aid your score.

Enjoy the Credit Strength of Others

You can also build your credit score by serving as an authorized user. If you have someone whose credit report is great and has an awesome credit history, you just need to get the person's approval to be added to the person's card as an authorized user. This makes you a beneficiary of the person's credit score. Your credit report will reflect the good history of the person you are using his or her credit card. At the same time, if the person whose credit card you use makes a late payment, it will reflect on your credit report. Hence, you've got to make the right choice on who you want to add you as an authorized user.

Keep old accounts

Your credit history also determines a lot about your credit score. Having a credit card that has lasted for several years will improve your credit score. So, if you have a credit card that you've been using for over ten years, don't bother closing the account as that will impact your credit report negatively in the short-term. If there is a need for you to get rid of a credit account, it is best you go for your newest card.

Ontime payment of your bill

Don't give room for late payment. It hampers your credit score greatly. Always make your payment as early as possible. Don't let your bill stay for too long before you make your payment. If there is a month you will be unable to pay early, be smart about it. There are certain bills you can afford to pay a bit late. Unlike your mortgage and credit card balances, you can afford to pay your cell providers and utilities a bit late. Your credit card provider and mortgage lender will most definitely report any late payment to the credit bureau. A good way to know an account you can pay late is to go to your credit report portal and click on *Accounts*. You will see some accounts listed. Look out for those that are not listed, and they don't usually appear on your credit report. These are best for you to pay late while you ensure you pay those on the list early enough. At the same time, note that this is a temporal strategy. Ensure you pay up all accounts early enough.

Using Goodwill Letter

A goodwill letter is what you need to wipe off a single mistake on a credit report. Does it sound so simple? Well, it is and it is not. It works if you have no record of default with your creditors before the mistake. The letter is a request you send to a bank or your lender to remove a missed or late payment from your report. It is called a *goodwill adjustment*. Note that the creditor is not under any obligation to approve your request. It lies in the discretion of the creditor to either approve or disapprove it. If you don't have a smooth history with your creditor, a goodwill letter is not an option for you to consider. Creditors will not be interested in granting the request.

When you need a Goodwill Letter

Writing a goodwill letter will help you correct mistakes in your credit report. But it doesn't work for all consumers. Creditors have their expectations as well. Below are possible cases that warrant the need to use a goodwill letter.

If you are faced with an emergency

Life is unpredictable, and there is nothing anyone can do about that. Even your creditors are aware of this truth. It may be an accident or a natural disaster that will make the payment of your balances a less priority. If this occurs, it is understandable that you write your creditors to help you remove the entry from your report.

Payment challenge

While it pays to make online payments because of their smoothness and secured manner of operations, it is also possible to experience glitches with your payment. There are times you make your payment, but it will fail to transmit. When such occurs, you need to write your creditor with proof. A blockage to your internet connection may be the cause. If you point these out, you will most likely be pardoned.

Mailing your bill to a wrong address

Many consumers end up making a payment late because their bills went to their former address. If your mail didn't reach your present location, you might end up paying late. So, this is a good reason for you to request a goodwill adjustment.

Once you've got a genuine reason(s) for making a late payment, it becomes easier for you to request a goodwill adjustment be made to your credit report. Although you have genuine reasons for requesting a goodwill adjustment, you've got to still follow some tips for you to write your letter.

Writing your Goodwill Letter

Here are some things you need to note as you write your goodwill letter.

Politeness is key: In your letter, avoid a negative tone. The creditor or your lender is never under any obligation to correct your mistake regardless of the reason for it. So, stay polite and calm.

Be straight to the point: You are not expected to write a novel. Just go straight into the reason you are writing. Let the lender know about what really happened by presenting your facts. Explain how the circumstances affected you in the payment of your bill. Don't wait so much time on it. You've got to maintain the fact and be concise enough.

Show the reasons: It is not enough to have good writing skills. You've got to know how to show. So, present evidence to back up your points. You may have to get some document from your insurance to show that you had issues, or maybe a medical report to show it was a medical issue. Just present what can be used to back up your claim. It will help your creditor or lender consider your request.

Don't just write, monitor: Writing and presenting evidence are not enough. If your letter doesn't reach the right person, then it is in vain. It is advised that you send your goodwill letter to the customer service agent (if it is a bank, but not the finance department). If it's possible, get it over to the manager of the organization.

Follow up your letter: I cannot emphasize this enough. You've got to follow up with your letter. You may not get an immediate response from your creditor, so wait for 30 days, and if you don't get any response, make a phone call or send an email.

Writing a goodwill letter will save your credit score a lot. You will not have to be concerned about specific possible issues you are likely to face with a messed up credit report. All it takes you to write an effective goodwill letter is to have enough evidence to prove that you did not miss the payment intentionally. Below is a sample of a goodwill letter you can use to make your request.

Sample Goodwill letter

[your name]

[your address]

Account Number: [your account number]

[date]

To Whom It May Concern:

Thank you for taking the time to read this letter. I'm writing because I noticed that my most recent credit report contains [a late payment/payments] reported on [date/dates] for my [name of account] account.

I want you to know that I understand my financial obligations, and if it weren't for [circumstance that caused you to miss a payment], I'd have an excellent repayment record. I made a mistake in falling behind, but since then, [description of how your circumstances have changed or how you've improved your money management]. Since then, I've had a spotless record of on-time payments.

I'm planning to apply for [a mortgage/auto loan/etc.], and it's come to my attention that the missed payment on my record could hurt my ability to qualify. I truly believe that it doesn't reflect my creditworthiness and commitment to repaying my debts. It would help me immensely if you could give me a second chance and make a goodwill adjustment to remove the late [payment/payments] on [date/dates].

Thank you for your consideration, and I hope you'll approve of my request.

Best, [your name]

Retrieved from
https://www.nerdwallet.com/article/finance/goodwill-letter

Chapter 7
MANAGING YOUR CREDIT CARD

Credit cards can be a convenient method to borrow if used rightly. However, if it is used otherwise, your debts will keep springing out of control because you are not paying off your balance in full or before the end of any promotional or 0% interest periods. Technology has made access to loan easier with an increase in the number of available credit cards for everyone.

Secured Credit Card

Secured cards are often sold to customers looking to build or rebuild their credit. Hence, the security deposit acts as a guarantee if you default on payments, but it's fully refundable if you pay off your balance in full and close your account. A secured credit card is almost the same as an unsecured credit card. Still, it is compulsory to make a minimum deposit (known as a security deposit) to collect a credit limit. The warranty is typically $200 or more depending on the secured card you open.

How Secured Credit Cards Work

Before you can start using your secured card, just like any other credit card, you will make the minimum security deposit ($200). You are allowed to spend up to your credit limit (it is often equal to your security deposit). If you want to increase your spending power, you will need to deposit more money.

Unsecured Credit Card

The unsecured credit card is mainly the common type of credit card that is not secured with collateral. The issuer does not have a security deposit they can take if you do not pay your credit card balance. However, the creditor's alternatives are to take advance collection efforts.

How Unsecured Credit Cards Work

Since unsecured credit cards involve no collateral, so the conditions of the debt are based on the borrower's credit application information, ability to pay, rating, and other factors. Since the debt is unsecured, this kind of debt is naturally somewhat riskier for lenders to issue. Most credit unions, banks, and other financial services providers offer unsecured credit cards. But to get one, you must apply with your details and agreement to a credit check. If your request is approved for an unsecured credit account, you will be given a card that you can use online, in stores, and over the phone for purchases.

Choosing the Right Credit Card

Getting a credit card can be demanding, yet, you have to choose wisely and apply with care. There are several credit card issuers. Choose the best card that will suit your financial needs and capacity. To do this, take note of the following:

Check the Annual Percentage Rate (APR): The annual percentage rate (APR) quantifies the card's total cost. However, it would be best if you used it with care. The way the APR is calculated is laid down in law and is based on definite norms. How much you spend on it each month, on purchases or other transactions, and how much you repay depends on how you use the card. The APR assumes that you use it only for purchases and can not consider the cost of balance transfers and cash withdrawals. It also ignores any introductory rates.

Check the Representative Percentage Rate (APR): What you see is not frequently what you acquire. Some card providers set your interest rate based on your credit record. This simply means that, if you do not have a good credit rating, you might pay a complex ratio of interest, and so the APR might be higher than what is publicized. Advertising/publishing will usually appraise a representative APR to look like the most common one that people (at least 51% or better) are offered.

Check the fees: Check out the other charges that are attached to your use of the card. Look out for the differences in the late payment rates and other possible charges you may have to bear. Choose a card that has low charges.

Compare introductory offers: Card providers regularly attract you with their offers that last for a fixed period. The most common is to pay 0% interest on things you buy or balance transfers. In most cases, the 0% offer might not be for purchases and balance transfers, but usually, it is just on balance transfers, and the introductory periods might be different. Check and enquire the offer details.

Check the terms and conditions: Enquire about the terms and conditions on a balance transfer. A balance transfer means transferring debt from one credit card to the other. There are many reasonable introductory offers, but check how long these last. You must pay a fee, most likely 3% of the balance transferred; this needs to be put into considerations. Again, check out for the transfer's time limit to meet up minimum payment to avoid withdrawal of the 0% offer.

Check monthly payment: If you are not paying back in full monthly, you can use the Credit card calculator to know how much interest you would end up paying. The amount can be frightening unless you are on a 0% offer or have more costly debts elsewhere; otherwise, you should always target to pay off what you owe at the end of the month.

Now that you know the possible things to check out for when selecting credit cards, the next item is understanding how to use it correctly.

Using Your Credit Card Rightly

Most household debts originate from their use of credit cards. Many Americans are wallowing in bad debt because they have failed to use their credit cards correctly. If you can put your card to good use and maintain the right care with your spending, your credit score will soar, and your report will be filled with positive information.

Keeping your PIN secure: make sure you make your credit card PIN a secret. Don't share it with anyone else. In the case of fraudulent acts, banks do not pay back if you are at fault. Most times, a refund is made to victims who are not at fault. It is best to use a PIN that is easily remembered and challenging to guess. Avoid using your Date of birth, familiar numbers, and others that others could think of.

Checking your bill: Ensure your credit card statement is for things you bought. If otherwise, query anything you do not understand. If you get your credit card statement online, it is a good idea to check it on a specific day (say a week before the payment is due) so you get in the custom of ensuring everything is in order and that you pay it on time.

Avoid the late payment trap: If you do not pay your bill on or before its due time, there could be severe penalties like fees, problems getting another credit, and increased interest rates. However, there are ways you can avoid paying late such as pay by direct debit (debited by your bank account automatically) or pay with time to spare (online and phone).

Avoid minimum payment trap: The minimum amount you need to refund on your card monthly is usually relatively small but paying this amount will cost you a lot in the long run. Hence, you could be making refunds for years and still end up paying more interest.

Learn to Stay within your credit limit: Usually, you are charged up to $30 whenever you exceed your credit limit, and it is likely to affect your credit rating too. But if you must increase your credit limit, you should contact your card provider to request manually. Always consider your comfortability of refunding and not be tempted to spend more than necessary.

Avoid cash withdrawals: Unlike debit cards, you can not withdraw cash for free on Credit cards. You will be charged higher interest than usual, even if you pay off your card in full monthly as there is no interest-free period, unlike purchases. Some of the transactions treated as cash withdrawals are buying foreign currency, buying postal orders, competition entry fees, gambling transactions, etc.

Avoid recurrent payments: A recurrent expenditure, also known as continuous payment authority, allows the company to put the charges onto your credit card bill automatically. But this is not as safe as a direct debit from a bank account. You can contact your card provider to cancel a recurring payment by withdrawing your permission from the company to take payment. If payments are still taken after removing your authorization, the card provider must refund the money and all related charges to the cardholder. However, you have to notify them on or before the end of the previous working day.

Protecting your payments: There are measures (insurance) kept aside for those who lose their jobs or fall victim to natural phenomena, etc., in order to protect their payment. However, the insurance policy may be expensive, and their terms and conditions differ. Hence one has to think deeply before considering protecting payment.

Log into your account: One reason a credit card is more manageable to use is that it makes the process of keeping a record of expenses easier. If you use credit for your purchases, there is no need to keep receipts for gas and grocery purchases. Rather, you can log in to your online account to check the record of how much you spent, where money was spent, and your balance. There is a need to check always (once a week); it will help you place your spending attitude under control.

If you gain control over your credit card, you will have in-depth control over your finances. Your credit card has a lot of influence on you. Start using it right, and you will be amazed at how much you will see as a result.

Chapter 8
IDENTITY THEFT

Identity theft is a big challenge. The record shows that more than three million consumers filed identity theft complaints last year alone, according to the Federal Trade Commission. Identity theft is more difficult to identify unless you observe your credit reports often. To stop identity theft is even more challenging and involves informing authorities about contacting the credit bureaus, doubtful new accounts, and possibly freezing your credit reports.

Real identity theft happens when a fraudster acts like you and uses your details (name, address, Social Security number, etc.) to register credit lines in your name. The best way to prevent identity theft is to regularly check your credit report by logging in to your account. This includes you checking bills and emails relating to your account as they are being forwarded to you. A victim of identity theft will likely find himself or herself being denied access to credit due to credit issues he or she doesn't know about.

Preventing Identity Theft

Identity theft can create chaos on your credit records and your entire financial comfort, but it is not the end of the world. Credit card provider naturally gives $0 fraud liability policies when you report unauthorized fees on time.

Frequently check your credit reports and account statements: Take the time to monitor your three credit reports occasionally for anything suspicious. The credit bureaus provide free credit reports once a year. Try not to throw aside the account statements and bills received. If any unusual charges or activities are discovered, contact your creditor to validate charges.

Keep your cards secured: Credit cards are the primary targets for fraud/criminals, so it is essential to build a good habit of keeping your details private. Avoid carrying pictures of your credit cards around in your phone, and keep your credit cards locked up in a safe place at home or in your wallet.

Using virtual credit card numbers: You can check with your credit card provider to see if it provides virtual credit card numbers. They are like digital versions of credit cards and are usually used for online shopping to avoid credit card fraud and identity theft. If your virtual card information is compromised, you can cancel it without affecting your existing card account.

Dealing with Identity Theft

The best time to deal with identity theft is when it has not occurred. It will be too late for you to deal with identity theft when your card already became prey in the hands of fraudsters. All you can do then is to take on a defensive posture and take your time to control the damage done. Hence, it is best to prevent the occurrence, and with the help of the Fair Credit Reporting Act (FCRA), there are some widespread protection measures against identity theft.

Prevent further damage: The first step to take from more fraudulent accounts from being open in your name is to place a credit restriction on your three credit reports. Credit locks are another alternative with a similar effect, though this may come with attached fees or strings. However, credit freezing is free and takes your credit report out of circulation, and avoid new creditors from receiving a copy of your information without your authorization. After placing a credit freeze, you have to defrost your credit reports, courtesy of a PIN you are issued by each credit bureau, before applying for new credit.

File an identity theft report: As a victim of identity theft, filing a report should be at the top of your priority. For any report to be considered as an identity theft report, it must have been officially filed with a law enforcement agency (fraud or police report). The report will be used to get any other fraudulent accounts removed from your credit information.

Contact the police if compulsory: After filing your report with a law enforcement agency, your recovery plan would tell you if you should contact the police or not. Identity theft is a big crime, and you may feel like reporting the situation to the police as a start. However, bear in mind that police naturally have a lot going on. If the police are not showing interest in taking your report, your state attorney general should be contacted.

Dispute fraud with the credit bureaus: You can submit disputes to the three major credit bureaus. If the fraudulent activities continue to show up (True name fraud), you will get your official identity theft report from the FTC or residential police department, including your disputes. The credit bureaus will then block all fraudulent accounts from your credit report, usually within four business days.

With the above measures, you can deal and stop identity theft from your credit card.

CHAPTER 9
DISPUTING INADEQUACIES IN YOUR REPORT

Your credit report contains vital information about you, such as your address, how you make your bill payment if you have been sued, arrested, or convicted for any crime, file for bankruptcy, and a lot more. This important information is sold out by credit reporting companies to your creditors, employers, insurers, and other institutions who want to examine your applications for a home, insurance, or a loan. The privacy of this vital information about you is guarded by The Federal Fair Credit Reporting Act (FCRA).

It is highly advised that you examine your credit report thoroughly and often because of the following reasons:

1. The vital information in your credit report will ascertain if you would receive loans from financial institutions or not.
2. To protect you against purloining whereby an individual makes use of your private details such as – name, credit card number, and social

security number to steal. Fraudsters may also use the vital information they have received to open new bank accounts in your name so that when they are in debt, it is your account that is reported because the account was registered in your name. This has a grave impact, particularly-on your financial life, as you might not be able to pay bills, apply for loans, job, or buy a car.
3. To ensure that the information contained in your credit report is accurate and updated if you want to buy a car, take a loan, or apply for a job.

How Do You Order for a Free Credit report?

Equifax, Experian, and TransUnion are the Nationwide credit reporting companies that have been demanded by the FCRA to give you a free credit report whenever you request once every twelve months. These Nationwide credit reporting companies have one website, toll-free telephone number, and mailing address so you can request your free credit report once a year. To request your free annual report, visit annualcreditreport.com or call 1-877-322-8228 or mail your complete Annual Credit Report Request Form to:

Annual Credit Report Request Service

P.O. Box 105281

Atlanta, GA 30348-5281

Note that none of these Nationwide Credit Reporting Companies should be contacted separately. You can request your free credit report from any of these three companies at the same time, or you can request from just one or two of the three companies. You would provide your name, Social Security number, Date of birth, and address. If you have relocated within the last two years, you should provide your previous address too. To ensure the security of your file, each nationwide reporting company may request different personal information exclusive to you.

You can also make a free report if a company takes harsh steps against you. For instance, they deny you a job, insurance, or application for credit due to the vital details in your report. Note that it is mandatory that you request a report within 60 days of notice. The notice of action would contain location details of the credit reporting company, such as their name, address, and phone number.

You can also request a free credit report if you plan to start job hunting within the subsequent sixty days or if your report is not accurate due to identity theft or fraud; you can also request a free credit report if you are welcome. A credit reporting company may charge you if you request a second credit report within 12 months. To buy a credit report, get in touch with these credit report companies:

TransUnion-1-800-916-8800

www.transunion.com

Experian-1-888-397-3742

www.experian.com

Equifax-1-800-685-1111

www.equifax.com

Correct Inadequacies in Credit Report

The credit reporting company, the person, company, or organization that gave information about you are responsible for correcting any inadequacies that might be found in your credit report under FCRA; therefore, make use of this right by getting in touch with the credit reporting company and information provider.

FIRST STEP

State the information you think is inaccurate in your dispute letter to the credit reporting company. Add duplicates of documents to back up this claim. After stating your name and address, your letter should identify each part of your report you do not agree on, include facts and discuss why you do not agree and request that the inaccurate information be corrected or excluded from the report. Send your dispute letter through certified mail, 'return receipt requested,' so you can write what credit the company got. Ensure to save all copies of your dispute letter and enclosures. Credit reporting companies' investigation lasts for about thirty days, only if they think your dispute is suspicious. The credit reporting company sends your dispute letter to the information provider, and it examines and investigates the claims and sends a report to the credit reporting company. After this, the credit reporting company communicates with the three nationwide credit reporting companies to correct the information on your file if they discover that the information on your credit report is indeed inaccurate.

The credit reporting company provides the results of the completed investigation in writing and a free copy of your report if there are changes in the dispute report. The credit reporting company also sends a written notice that contains: your name, address, and phone number of the person, organization that provided the information. On request, the credit company sends notices of the corrections to any persons, organizations, or companies that may have seen your report within the past six months.

If the dispute is not resolved by the credit reporting company, you can request that statement of the dispute be added to your file and in a subsequent report. You will most likely pay for this.

Second Step

Inform the person or company that provided the information about you to the credit report company in writing that you do not agree to an aspect of your dispute report. Add duplicated copies of documents to back up your claim and send the letter to the address of the information provider (provided it is in your credit report). However, if the address of the information provider is not included in your credit report, contact the provider and request for an address; if the provider does not send an address, transfer the letter to any business address for the provider.

If the information provider keeps giving incorrect information about you to a credit reporting company, it is a must for your dispute to be stated if your claims are accurate. If your claims are not accurate, the information provider needs to contact the credit reporting company to exclude your claims.

In conclusion, a credit report has to be accurate and up-to-date as it is quite essential to your financial life. It is, therefore, important that you review your credit report on a regular basis so you can identify errors (if any) and report inadequacies through the steps provided.

SAMPLE OF A DISPUTE LETTER

[Your Name]
[Your Address]
[Your City, State, Zip Code]

[Date]

Complaint Department
[Company Name]
[Street Address]
[City, State, Zip Code]

Dear Sir or Madam:

I am writing to dispute the following information in my file. I have circled the items I dispute on the attached copy of the report I received.

This item [identify the item(s) disputed by the name of the sources, such as creditors or tax court, and identify the type of item, such as credit account, judgment, etc.] is [inaccurate or

incomplete] because [**describe what is inaccurate or incomplete and why**]. I am requesting that the item be removed [**or request another specific change**] to correct the information.

Enclosed are copies of [**use this sentence if applicable and describe any enclosed documentation, such as payment records and court documents**] supporting my position. Please reinvestigate this [**these**] matter[**s**] and [**delete or correct**] the disputed item[**s**] as soon as possible.

Sincerely,
Your name

Retrieved from

https://www.consumer.ftc.gov/articles/0384-sample-letter-disputing-errors-your-credit-report

Conclusion

Your credit score is the coach of your life. It determines the level to which you can achieve your financial goals. Building a good credit score has to do with you learning the right financial habits. Ensure you pay your balance early enough, keep a long credit history, and keep a good credit utilization ratio. Managing your credit card is another step you've got to take if you want to fill your credit report with positive information. A man who rules his credit card is above major financial issues of life, but the man who allows his credit card to rule him is totally subjected to the rule of financial challenges. Take a stance and build your credit score to reach your financial goals.

www.ingramcontent.com/pod-product-compliance
Lightning Source LLC
Chambersburg PA
CBHW070451220526
45466CB00004B/1799

9798584888404